All The Reasons The St. Louis Cardinals Are Better Than The Kansas City Royals

All The Reasons The

St. Louis Cardinals

Are Better Than The

Kansas City Royals

A Comprehensive Analysis Of All Of The Superior Qualities Of The Cardinals Compared To The Royals

Jeff Slutsky

STREET FIGHTER PRESS

PRESS

All The Reasons The St. Louis Cardinals Are
Better Than The Kansas City Royals

To order this book on line: https://www.allthereasons.net

ISBN-13: 978-1530578276
ISBN-10: 1530578272

Dedication

This book is dedicated to the fans of the World Champion Kansas City Royals.

ALSO AVAILABLE BY BY JEFF SLUTSKY

All The Reasons The K-State Wildcats Are Better Than
The Kansas Jayhawks

All The Reasons The Missouri Tigers Are Better Than
The Kansas Jayhawks

All The Reasons The Green Bay Packers Are Better Than
The Chicago Bears

All the Reasons The Minnesota Vikings Are Better Than
The Green Bay Packers

All The Reasons The LSU Tigers Are Better Than
The Alabama Crimson Tide

All The Reasons The Minnesota Golden Gophers
Are Better Than The Wisconsin Badgers

All The Reasons Michigan Is Better Than Ohio State

All The Reasons The Army Black Knights Are Better Than
The Navy Midshipment

All The Reasons To Love Obamacare

All The Reasons I Love Accounting

Some More Serious Books By Jeff Slutsky

More Smart Marketing

Smart Selling

From The Big Screen to the Real World

Totastmaster's Guide To Successful Speaking

Street Fighter Marketing for Your Business

Street Fighter Marketing Solutions

No B.S. Grassroots Marketing

To order books - https://www.allthereasons.net

THIS PAGE IS BLANK DUE TO LACK OF REASONS

THIS PAGE IS BLANK DUE
TO LACK OF REASONS

THIS PAGE IS BLANK DUE TO LACK OF REASONS

THIS PAGE IS BLANK DUE
TO LACK OF REASONS

THIS PAGE IS BLANK DUE TO LACK OF REASONS

THIS PAGE IS BLANK DUE TO LACK OF REASONS

THIS PAGE IS BLANK DUE TO LACK OF REASONS

If you think this book gets better, you will be vastly disappointed. But go ahead, keep reading.

THIS PAGE IS BLANK DUE
TO LACK OF REASONS

THIS PAGE IS BLANK DUE TO LACK OF REASONS

THIS PAGE IS BLANK DUE
TO LACK OF REASONS

THIS PAGE IS BLANK DUE TO LACK OF REASONS

THIS PAGE IS BLANK DUE
TO LACK OF REASONS

THIS PAGE IS BLANK DUE
TO LACK OF REASONS

THIS PAGE IS BLANK DUE
TO LACK OF REASONS

Here's a reason! Whoops. I was wrong. Keep
reading. Something may come up.

THIS PAGE IS BLANK DUE TO LACK OF REASONS

THIS PAGE IS BLANK DUE
TO LACK OF REASONS

THIS PAGE IS BLANK DUE
TO LACK OF REASONS

THIS PAGE IS BLANK DUE
TO LACK OF REASONS

THIS PAGE IS BLANK DUE TO LACK OF REASONS

THIS PAGE IS BLANK DUE
TO LACK OF REASONS

THIS PAGE IS BLANK DUE TO LACK OF REASONS

THIS PAGE IS BLANK DUE
TO LACK OF REASONS

THIS PAGE IS BLANK DUE
TO LACK OF REASONS

THIS PAGE IS BLANK DUE
TO LACK OF REASONS

Do you have a friend who is a St. Louis Cardinals
fan? Make their day. Buy them a copy of this book.

THIS PAGE IS BLANK DUE
TO LACK OF REASONS

THIS PAGE IS BLANK DUE
TO LACK OF REASONS

THIS PAGE IS BLANK DUE
TO LACK OF REASONS

THIS PAGE IS BLANK DUE
TO LACK OF REASONS

THIS PAGE IS BLANK DUE TO LACK OF REASONS

THIS PAGE IS BLANK DUE
TO LACK OF REASONS

THIS PAGE IS BLANK DUE TO LACK OF REASONS

THIS PAGE IS BLANK DUE
TO LACK OF REASONS

THIS PAGE IS BLANK DUE TO LACK OF REASONS

THIS PAGE IS BLANK DUE
TO LACK OF REASONS

THIS PAGE IS BLANK DUE TO LACK OF REASONS

Fun Fact: Every book in this series received 1 out of 5 stars from Amazon. One buyer bought the Minnisota Vikings/Green Bay Packers book for her husband (a huge Vikings fan) and commented that it actually "ruined her Christmas."

With your help, this book could get an even lower rating! Go on Amazon.com today and give it the worse rating possible. Thanks.

THIS PAGE IS BLANK DUE
TO LACK OF REASONS

THIS PAGE IS BLANK DUE
TO LACK OF REASONS

THIS PAGE IS BLANK DUE
TO LACK OF REASONS

THIS PAGE IS BLANK DUE TO LACK OF REASONS

THIS PAGE IS BLANK DUE
TO LACK OF REASONS

THIS PAGE IS BLANK DUE TO LACK OF REASONS

THIS PAGE IS BLANK DUE TO LACK OF REASONS

THIS PAGE IS BLANK DUE TO LACK OF REASONS

THIS PAGE IS BLANK DUE
TO LACK OF REASONS

THIS PAGE IS BLANK DUE TO LACK OF REASONS

THIS PAGE IS BLANK DUE
TO LACK OF REASONS

Fun Fact: My good friend Dan Wolt owns an online window replacement company franchise called Zen Windows. To help him increase the response rate for the proposals that he mails out, I created book for him which his prospects receive a couple days after they get their bids. *All The Reasons NOT To Buy From Zen Windows.* His response rate doubled! Now I haved all new windows in my house.

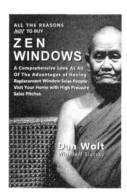

THIS PAGE IS BLANK DUE
TO LACK OF REASONS

THIS PAGE IS BLANK DUE TO LACK OF REASONS

THIS PAGE IS BLANK DUE TO LACK OF REASONS

THIS PAGE IS BLANK DUE
TO LACK OF REASONS

THIS PAGE IS BLANK DUE
TO LACK OF REASONS

THIS PAGE IS BLANK DUE
TO LACK OF REASONS

THIS PAGE IS BLANK DUE
TO LACK OF REASONS

THIS PAGE IS BLANK DUE
TO LACK OF REASONS

THIS PAGE IS BLANK DUE TO LACK OF REASONS

THIS PAGE IS BLANK DUE
TO LACK OF REASONS

THIS PAGE IS BLANK DUE TO LACK OF REASONS

THIS PAGE IS BLANK DUE
TO LACK OF REASONS

THIS PAGE IS BLANK DUE TO LACK OF REASONS

THIS PAGE IS BLANK DUE
TO LACK OF REASONS

THIS PAGE IS BLANK DUE TO LACK OF REASONS

THIS PAGE IS BLANK DUE
TO LACK OF REASONS

THIS PAGE IS BLANK DUE TO LACK OF REASONS

THIS PAGE IS BLANK DUE
TO LACK OF REASONS

THIS PAGE IS BLANK DUE TO LACK OF REASONS

THIS PAGE IS BLANK DUE
TO LACK OF REASONS

THIS PAGE IS BLANK DUE TO LACK OF REASONS

THIS PAGE IS BLANK DUE
TO LACK OF REASONS

THIS PAGE IS BLANK DUE TO LACK OF REASONS

THIS PAGE IS BLANK DUE
TO LACK OF REASONS

THIS PAGE IS BLANK DUE TO LACK OF REASONS

THIS PAGE IS BLANK DUE
TO LACK OF REASONS

THIS PAGE IS BLANK DUE TO LACK OF REASONS

THIS PAGE IS BLANK DUE
TO LACK OF REASONS

THIS PAGE IS BLANK DUE TO LACK OF REASONS

THIS PAGE IS BLANK DUE
TO LACK OF REASONS

THIS PAGE IS BLANK DUE TO LACK OF REASONS

THIS PAGE IS BLANK DUE
TO LACK OF REASONS

THIS PAGE IS BLANK DUE TO LACK OF REASONS

THIS PAGE IS BLANK DUE
TO LACK OF REASONS

THIS PAGE IS BLANK DUE TO LACK OF REASONS

THIS PAGE IS BLANK DUE
TO LACK OF REASONS

THIS PAGE IS BLANK DUE TO LACK OF REASONS

THIS PAGE IS BLANK DUE TO LACK OF REASONS

THIS PAGE IS BLANK DUE TO LACK OF REASONS

THIS PAGE IS BLANK DUE
TO LACK OF REASONS

THIS PAGE IS BLANK DUE TO LACK OF REASONS

THIS PAGE IS BLANK DUE
TO LACK OF REASONS

THIS PAGE IS BLANK DUE TO LACK OF REASONS

JEFF SLUTSKY   WWW.ALLTHEREASONS.NET

THIS PAGE IS BLANK DUE TO LACK OF REASONS

THIS PAGE IS BLANK DUE
TO LACK OF REASONS

THIS PAGE IS BLANK DUE
TO LACK OF REASONS

THIS PAGE IS BLANK DUE
TO LACK OF REASONS

THIS PAGE IS BLANK DUE
TO LACK OF REASONS

THIS PAGE IS BLANK DUE
TO LACK OF REASONS

THIS PAGE IS BLANK DUE
TO LACK OF REASONS

THIS PAGE IS BLANK DUE
TO LACK OF REASONS

THIS PAGE IS BLANK DUE
TO LACK OF REASONS

THIS PAGE IS BLANK DUE TO LACK OF REASONS

THIS PAGE IS BLANK DUE TO LACK OF REASONS

THIS PAGE IS BLANK DUE TO LACK OF REASONS

THIS PAGE IS BLANK DUE
TO LACK OF REASONS

THIS PAGE IS BLANK DUE TO LACK OF REASONS

THIS PAGE IS BLANK DUE
TO LACK OF REASONS

THIS PAGE IS BLANK DUE TO LACK OF REASONS

THIS PAGE IS BLANK DUE
TO LACK OF REASONS

THIS PAGE IS BLANK DUE TO LACK OF REASONS

THIS PAGE IS BLANK DUE
TO LACK OF REASONS

THIS PAGE IS BLANK DUE TO LACK OF REASONS

THIS PAGE IS BLANK DUE
TO LACK OF REASONS

THIS PAGE IS BLANK DUE TO LACK OF REASONS

THIS PAGE IS BLANK DUE
TO LACK OF REASONS

THIS PAGE IS BLANK DUE TO LACK OF REASONS

THIS PAGE IS BLANK DUE
TO LACK OF REASONS

THIS PAGE IS BLANK DUE TO LACK OF REASONS

THIS PAGE IS BLANK DUE
TO LACK OF REASONS

THIS PAGE IS BLANK DUE TO LACK OF REASONS

THIS PAGE IS BLANK DUE
TO LACK OF REASONS

THIS PAGE IS BLANK DUE TO LACK OF REASONS

THIS PAGE IS BLANK DUE TO LACK OF REASONS

THIS PAGE IS BLANK DUE TO LACK OF REASONS

THIS PAGE IS BLANK DUE
TO LACK OF REASONS

THIS PAGE IS BLANK DUE TO LACK OF REASONS

To order more copies of this book on line:
https://www.allthereasons.net
Also Available:

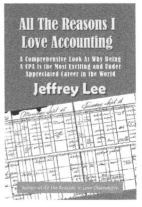

To order *More Smart Marketing:*

www.createspace.com/4403184

To order *Smart Selling:*

www.createspace.com/4411673

Made in the USA
Monee, IL
11 October 2022

15654849R00075